TASTES of
Charles Island

Marissa D'Angelo

Copyright © 2024 Marissa D'Angelo
ISBN: 9798990430983
All rights reserved. This publication may not be reproduced, distributed, or transmitted in any form or by any means, including photocopying, recording, or other electronic or mechanical means, without the prior written permission of the publisher, except in the case of brief quotations embodied in critical reviews and certain other noncommercial uses permitted by copyright law.
Cover design by Amy Hunter

Printed in the United States of America.

DEDICATION

This book is dedicated to my family. Thank you for passing on your traditions to me. This book wouldn't have been possible without you all.

Table of Contents

Breakfast

HOMEFRIES	1-2
EGGS IN A NEST	3
BLUEBERRY BUCKLE	4
AVOCADO TOAST	5
CHUNKY MONKEY BANANA MUFFINS	6
BREAKFAST PIE	7-8
HAM & CHEESE SANDWICH	9

Lunch/Dinner

SALMON IN CREAM SAUCE	13-14
BLACKENED SALMON	15
MEAT LOVERS PIZZA	16
BACON CHICKEN	17-18
SLOW COOKED BEEF	19
CHICKEN ROAST WITH GRAVY	21-22
CHICKEN FRANCAISE	23
MARGHERITA PIZZA	25

Lunch/Dinner Continued

CHICKEN & SHRIMP SCAMPI	26
GNOCCHI	27-28
TURKEY & RICE MEAL PREP	29
BAKED ZITI	31
STUFFED PEPPERS	32
KEILBASA & POTATOES	33
BBQ CHICKEN	35-36
SLOW COOKED CHILI	37

Lunch/Dinner Continued

CHICKEN PARMIGIANA	38
CHICKEN CUTLET	41-42
CHICKEN SOUP	43-44
PULLED CHICKEN TACOS	45
GUACAMOLE	46
PEPPERONI BREAD	47
GRILLED CHEESE	48
BROCCOLI CASSEROLE	49

Dessert

WILDBERRY COBBLER	53
CHOCOLATE CHIP COOKIES	54
PEPPERMINT CANDY CANE CAKE	55
DOG TREATS	56

Breakfast

The Story of Homefries

"You've got to use bacon fat!" Grandma hollered from her fridge. I remember my face going completely green as I thought *Bacon Fat? That's disgusting! Why would I want to put that in my delicious breakfast potatoes?* She got a spoonful while I looked away and placed it in the pan with the diced potatoes.

"Well, now we can't eat it!" I had said.

"This adds the flavor!" she laughed. I thought about how yummy bacon was and decided to let the idea enter my mind that this could actually turn out well.

"Remember the hungarian recipe, szalonnasütés? We put bacon fat over rye bread. You can even use the bacon fat for your grilled cheese! Watch and you shall see..." she said, letting her E's trail like she was singing a song. She talked like this sometimes, but especially when she would cook. I flipped over the homefries again and again, making sure all sides were a nice, deep brown color. Grandma was in charge of the eggs because whenever I was, I couldn't help but eat most of the cheese before putting it in with the scrambled eggs. She had found out my secret. I tried a bite of the homefries.

"I think these are the best homefries I have ever had," I couldn't wait to pour them on my plate and ended up eating them right from the pan.

"Told ya!" grandma said.

Homefries

Ingredients :

- 4-5 potatoes
- 1/4 onion (diced)
- 1 tbsp garlic (minced)
- salt and pepper
- 1 tbsp paprika
- olive oil or vegetable oil
- bacon grease (optional)

Prep Time : 10 min

Cook Time : 20 min

Servings : 4

Procedure :

1. Dice potatoes and keep skin on; run through water in a strainer to get starch out for about 30 seconds
2. Put potatoes in a pot of water to boil (watch closely; only boil for about 5-6 minutes)
3. While the potatoes are cooking, sautee onions and garlic in large saucepan with oil. If you have bacon grease, it adds a lot of flavor to the potatoes -- you can use this in addition to the oil. Cook on low to medium heat

- Strain potatoes in sink and add them to saucepan.
- Sprinkle 1 tbsp of paprika over potatoes. Salt and pepper to your liking
- Cook for about 10 minutes, flipping potatoes over to crisp both sides
- Enjoy next to some scrambled eggs and bacon!

Eggs in a Nest

Prep Time : 10 min

Cook Time : 20 min

Servings : 4

Ingredients :

- 2 slices of bread
- 2 eggs
- 3 tbsp butter

Procedure :

1. Heat 1 tbsp butter in pan over medium heat
2. Use cup upside down to press down into each slice of bread to make a hole. Save the middles
3. Spread butter over both sides of bread and middles
4. Place onto heated saucepan
5. Crack an egg in each hole
6. Cook for about 2 minutes on each side; careful not to cook too long or the egg will no longer be runny
7. Carefully flip onto other side
8. Serve next to bacon or sausage and diced avocado

Blueberry Buckle

Ingredients :

- 3/4 cups sugar
- 1 egg
- 2 cups flour
- 1/2 tsp salt
- 1/4 cup soft butter
- 1/2 cups milk
- 2 tsp baking powder
- 2 cups blueberries

Procedure :

1. Mix sugar, butter, and eggs. Stir in milk
2. Sift together dry ingredients and stir into mixture
3. Gently fold in blueberries
4. Top with crumb mix
5. Pour in greased 9x13 inch pan. Bake 45 min in 350F oven

Crumb Mixture:

1/2 cups sugar, 1/3 cups flour, 1/2 tsp cinnamon and 1/4 cups soft butter.

Mix until crumbly.

Prep Time : 10 min

Cook Time : 20 min

Servings : 4

Avocado Toast

Ingredients :

- One ripe avocado
- Two slices of bread (any kind; I use honey wheat)
- 2 tbsp butter
- Salt & Pepper

Procedure :

1. Toast two slices of bread to your liking
2. Spread butter on each slice right away so it can melt slightly while it is warm
3. Cut avocado in half and take out pit
4. Using spoon, scoop out one half of the avocado onto one slice of bread and do the same with the other
5. Using fork, spread avocado on toast, gently mashing
6. Season with salt & pepper

Prep Time : 5 min

Cook Time : 2 min

Servings : 1

Chunky Monkey Banana Muffins

Prep Time : 10 min
Cook Time : 15-20 min
Servings : 4

Ingredients :

- 1/2 cup unsalted butter, softened
- 2/3 cup granulated sugar
- 2 large eggs
- 4 bananas, very ripe
- 1 tsp vanilla extract
- 4 tbsp peanut butter
- 1 1/2 cups all-purpose flour
- 1 tsp baking soda
- 1/2 tsp salt
- 1/2 tsp cinnamon
- 1/2 tsp honey
- 1 cup mini chocolate chips

Procedure :

1. Preheat oven to 350F and use cupcake liners to line muffin pan
2. In a medium mixing bowl, cream together 8 tbsp softened butter and 2/3 cup sugar. Add 2 eggs
3. Add 4 mashed bananas, 1 tsp vanilla extract, 1/2 tsp honey and 4 tbsp peanut butter. Mix
4. In separate small bowl, whisk together dry ingredients: 1 1/2 cups flour, 1 tsp baking soda, 1/2 tsp salt and 1/2 tsp cinnamon
5. Mix dry into wet ingredients. Fold chocolate chips in, leaving some for the topping of each muffin
6. Pour filling into each muffin cup, about 3/4 way up
7. Use the leftover chips to sprinkle over the top of each muffin prior to going in the oven
8. Bake 15-20 minutes (or until toothpick comes out clean)

The Story of the Breakfast Pie

Every time I'd stay over Nonni's house, the last thing I ever had to worry about was a good meal. It was custom for my family to always make sure that we served our guests with not just any food, but some delicious home-made goods. I slept over my Nonni & Nonno's house on many occasions, but this one time Nonni told me that she had something special for me to try the next morning.

"I'm not going to tell you what's in it, you'll have to guess!" She said.

I had been skeptical of trying it, wondering what could possibly be in this pie. But I took Nonni's word and tried it. A breakfast all in one was the first thing I could think of. Before I could say anything more, I went to the counter to grab another slice of the pie.

"I guess it's good, huh?" She had said while I already had my mouth full with seconds. The next time I slept over, she wanted to teach me how to make it with her. I suggested Italian sausage instead of breakfast sausage and the flavors came to life even more.

Now every time I go to Nonni's house…and this is about a decade later, she makes the delicious breakfast pie, but now in bite-size muffins. They're the perfect mix of ingredients to leave you feeling energized to start your day.

Breakfast Pie

Ingredients :

- 1 package sweet italian sausage
- 1 cup chopped red and green bell peppers
- 1/2 cup diced onion
- 3 cups frozen hash brown patties
- 2 1/2 cups shredded cheddar cheese (8 oz)
- 1 cup Bisquick pancake mix
- 2 cups milk
- 1/4 tsp pepper
- 4 eggs

Prep Time : 30 min

Cook Time : 35 min

Servings : 8

Procedure :

1. Preheat oven to 400F. Grease two 9 inch pie plates or a 13x9 inch pan
2. In skillet, cook sausage; drain and set aside when cooked all the way through
3. Sautee bell pepper and onion over medium heat for 10 minutes
4. Pour sausage, bell pepper and onion mixture in a bowl. Add diced hashbrown patties. (May want to keep hashbrown patties out for an hour to thaw to make it easier to dice)
5. Add 1 1/2 cups of cheese and mix. Pour in pie plates
6. In medium bowl, whisk bisquick mix, milk, pepper and eggs. Pour over sausage mixture in pie pans.
7. Bake 35-40 minutes or until knife in center comes out clean. Sprinkle with remaining cheese. Set aside for at least 10 minutes before eating

Ham & Cheese Sandwich

Ingredients :

- Ham Steak (diced)
- 2 eggs
- croissant or your choice of bread
- 1/4 cup cheddar cheese
- 1 tbsp butter
- salt & pepper

Prep Time : 30 min

Cook Time : 35 min

Servings : 8

Procedure :

1. In medium saucepan, melt butter
2. Crack 2 eggs in a bowl and add a drip of water
3. Whisk eggs, adding salt & pepper to season
4. Pour eggs in saucepan, flipping over when cooked
5. When eggs are just about cooked all the way through, add in cheese and diced hamsteak. Let cheese melt and scoop onto each croissant half

Lunch/Dinner

"When I headed back onto the ship to set sail for another voyage, I took on the job as an apprentice cook. Having never cooked before, I learned from Jack who was actually quite good at baiting fish in from the seas and frying them up."

-The Cursed Vessel

The Story of Salmon in Cream Sauce

"Nonni, you have a bunch of salmon in your fridge," I noticed when I opened up her fridge on one of my visits.

"Oh...Uncle Vinny bought them. He wants to know if you'll cook up the salmon dish that you like to make. He won't stop bothering me about it!" Nonni said.

I knew it before I had even asked. I always liked an excuse to make this dish because it was one of my favorites.

"Let's have him over tomorrow night!" I exclaimed.

The next day, I showed Nonni how to make this dish and carefully flipped a bowl of cooked jasmine rice over on each plate.

"Okay, you pick your piece," I gestured over to Uncle Vinny. He chose to thickest piece while I liked the thin ones so it worked out. Using a spatula, I put each salmon fillet onto the plates. Then, for the best part... I took a spoonful of the creamy sauce with baby spinach and cherry tomatoes and drizzled it over the salmon fillet and rice.

"Here you go!" I set each plate down on the kitchen table.

"Gee, that looks even better than the last time! You'll have to teach me how to make it sometime," Uncle Vinny said.

"I'll do you one better, you can read my cookbook!"

Salmon in Cream Sauce

Prep Time : 15 min

Cook Time : 20 min

Servings : 4

Ingredients :

- 4 salmon fillets (skin on)
- salt and pepper
- 1 tbsp butter
- 3 cloves garlic (finely diced)
- 1 tsp paprika
- 1 1/2 cups cherry tomatoes
- 5 cups baby spinach
- 2 cups heavy cream
- 1/2 cup grated parmesan cheese
- 1/4 cup parsley

Procedure :

1. Sprinkle a dash of salt and pepper on salmon to season
2. Medium heat 1 tbsp oil
3. Cook salmon flesh side down first for about 5 minutes Flip salmon and cook on other side about 5 more minutes. Set aside
4. Add 1 tbsp butter and diced garlic to pan - cook 1 minute
5. Add 5 cups baby spinach. Let wilt
6. Reduce heat to low. Add 1 1/2 cups diced cherry tomatoes. Stir
7. Add 2 cups heavy cream, 1/2 cup parmesan cheese, parsley and paprika. Cover 5 minutes
8. Return salmon to pan soaking with spoon and cover on low for 5 minutes. Serve next to jasmine rice

Blackened Salmon

Ingredients :

- 4 salmon fillets (skin on)
- salt, pepper and paprika to season
- 1/2 tsp garlic powder, onion powder, cayenne pepper, dried oregano
- 1 tbsp olive oil
- 2 tbsp lime or lemon juice
- 1/4 cup chicken broth
- 3 tbsp butter
- 1-2 mandarin oranges

Prep Time : 10 min

Cook Time : 15 min

Servings : 4

Procedure :

1. Pour oil in cast iron pan & heat over medium heat
2. Season salmon with salt, pepper and paprika
3. Whisk garlic powder, onion powder, cayenne and dried oregano in a small bowl. Sprinkle over salmon to evenly coat surface
4. Place salmon flesh side down first. Cook 3-4 minutes
5. Flip to other side and let cook 3-4 minutes. Pour chicken broth into cast iron pan
6. Move salmon to plates & squeeze lime or lemon over salmon fillets
7. Peel and place pieces of mandarin oranges over each salmon fillet
8. Enjoy! Salmon is great next to jasmine rice

Meat Lovers Pizza

Ingredients :

- Pre-made dough (Wewalka Classic Pizza)
- 19 oz sweet italian sausage
- 1 ham steak, diced
- bacon
- 1/4 onion (diced)
- 2 roma tomatoes
- 1 cup mozzarella cheese
- 1/2 cup sauce
- 1 cup baby spinach

Procedure :

1. Preheat oven to 425°F
2. Lay out parchment paper over a circular pizza pan
3. Press pizza down onto pan; fold edges over to make a crust
4. Sautee onion & add baby spinach
5. Cook 1-2 italian sausages in a separate pan and chop into small pieces
6. Cook bacon and break into small pieces. Spread sauce over pizza
7. Sprinkle 1/2 cup cheese over sauce and sprinkle toppings
8. Sprinkle remaining 1/2 cup cheese over toppings
9. Bake 15-20 minutes or until edges are light brown

Prep Time : 20 min

Cook Time : 20 min

Servings : 4

The Story of Bacon Chicken

"Grandma, what are you doing??"

She smiled and hummed in response, continuing to rip apart bacon strips and place them onto each raw chicken slice. Surely she had lost her mind.

"If you're trying to make chicken cutlet, I'm pretty sure there's another way!" I suggested.

"You'll see, you'll see!! Get the duck sauce from the fridge," she gestured over to the fridge and I felt like I was in some kind of bizzarro world cartoon. *I might as well just go along with it*, I thought.

I looked through the fridge and finally found it in the side door; it was a huge jar of orange sauce with an Asian inscription on the front.

"Perfect," she said, seeing what I got out of the fridge. By then, she was already frying the chicken in oil on the stovetop. She took the jar from me and opened it up, spooning a bit onto each plate. When the chicken was done, she flipped them over in the pan and let it cook even more. She finally took one cooked piece out and cut a small bit off, dipping it into some of the duck sauce. She held the fork up to me.

"Try it, you might like it!!" She exclaimed as she always would with every new thing she made.

Bacon and chicken, what could possibly be bad about that? I thought. As soon as I tried it, I walked over to get the rest of the chicken and placed it on my plate, walking out of the room to finish it while grandma laughed in the kitchen, knowing full well I would be back for more.

Bacon Chicken

Ingredients :

- 1 package chicken cutlets (sliced thin)
- salt, pepper and paprika to season
- 1 package bacon
- flour
- 3 eggs
- oil

Prep Time : 5 min
Cook Time : 15 min
Servings   : 3

Procedure :

1. Heat oil in pan on medium heat.
2. While pan is heating, season chicken on both sides with salt, pepper and paprika
3. Cut each bacon strip in half and place a piece on each chicken cutlet
4. Dip chicken in egg then flour as a breading, ensuring the bacon stays on by keeping your fork in it
5. Fry chicken bacon-side down first until nice, golden brown color. Flip and cook other side
6. Let chicken drain on paper towel covered plate
7. Enjoy (a nice dipping sauce for this is Duck Sauce/sweet and sour sauce)

Slow Cooked Beef

Prep Time : 20 min

Cook Time : 6 hours

Servings : 4

Ingredients :

- 3 lb beef roast
- 2 cups beef broth
- 1/4 cup red wine
- 1 lb chopped carrots
- 4-5 potatoes (yellow or red)
- 1/2 onion (diced)
- 2 minced garlic cloves
- 2 tsp salt
- 1 tsp black pepper
- 1 tsp paprika
- 2 tsp garlic powder

Procedure :

1. Rinse beef roast and pat dry. Place in slow cooker
2. Chop carrots, potatoes and onion, placing into slow cooker beside beef.
3. Pour beef broth and red wine in slow cooker, over beef, carrots, potatoes and onion.
4. Cover beef with salt, pepper, paprika and garlic powder.
5. Poke 4 slits in top of beef with knife and put garlic cloves in each
6. Cover and cook on low 6 hours.
7. Enjoy next to some mashed potatoes, make sure to pour liquid over beef when serving

"They were to prepare the dishes for this evening. I haven't the slightest how to make everything," I mumbled.

"Hey, I know how to cook!" He blurted out. I couldn't help but smile at his suggestion. How would I be able to talk father into this?"

-The Cursed Inn

The Story of the Chicken Roast with Gravy

"Marissa, shhh she isn't looking," Dad said while he snuck the bacon strips off the chicken that was in the oven. He quickly put them on a plate and we tip toed over to the family room.

I couldn't help but laugh hysterically while gobbling up the bacon with dad. I was the worst thief.

"Marissa! Joey!!" Mom already must've discovered what we took. "Why did you steal all the bacon?!"

Dad and I just kept on laughing.

"Alright, I'll help you with the potatoes!" I called back in the kitchen and couldn't help but laugh even more when I saw mom's face, irritated at the both of us.

"We couldn't help it, it smelt so good!"

After I made the mashed potatoes and mom cut the chicken into slices, I set the table and called dad in to come eat with us. Mom made sure that dad and I both got some skin from the chicken and I had a bowl of my mashed potatoes right before us too. She made a swimming pool of the gravy over the potatoes.

Every Sunday, we had this feast together as a family. At the time, there weren't any cell-phones as they are today. But even so, without any distractions and just some delicious food before us and family, it was the perfect way to start the upcoming week. Remember to take time with your family and loved ones, distraction-free.

Chicken Roast with Gravy

Prep Time : 15 min

Cook Time : varies on lb

Servings : 4

Ingredients :

- Chicken Roast
- 1 tbsp butter
- 1 tbsp paprika
- 1 tsp salt
- 1 tsp pepper
- 1/4 cup white wine
- diced tomato
- diced onion
- 1 minced garlic clove
- 4 bacon strips

Gravy:
- 1 tbsp butter
- 1-4 tbsp flour
- chicken drippings

Procedure :

1. Prepare chicken by rinsing. If you'd like to brine overnight in a bowl of water with 3 tbsp salt, the chicken will be more moist. Place chicken in 13x9 inch baking pan
2. Melt 1 tbsp butter and add paprika, salt, pepper to bowl with butter. Stir thoroughly
3. Using spoon, drop spoonfuls of spice mixture over chicken
4. Put diced tomato, onion, garlic and wine around and inside chicken. Place bacon strips over top
5. Follow allotted time per lb of chicken. Cut thickest part beside cavity; if liquid is clear then chicken is done
6. When finished, let sit for at least 20 minutes before cutting

Gravy:
1. Strain drippings from roast chicken
2. Combine with 1 tbsp flour at a time with butter after cooked at low heat on stove

(Optional) Add cream of mushroom soup

Chicken Francaise

Ingredients :

- 1 package boneless, skinless chicken breasts (thinly sliced, 1/2 inch thick)
- salt, pepper & paprika
- 1 cup flour
- 1 tsp garlic powder
- 1/2 tsp paprika
- 3 tbsp butter
- 2 eggs
- 1/4 cup grated Parmigiano cheese
- 2 lemons
- 2 tbsp lemon juice
- 1/4 cup olive oil
- 2 cloves garlic, minced
- 1/2 cup white wine
- 1 cup chicken stock
- Linguine pasta

Prep Time : 15 min
Cook Time : 15 min
Servings : 4

Procedure :

1. Season chicken cutlets with salt, pepper and paprika on both sides. Season flour with garlic powder and paprika
2. Roll 3 tbsp (sliced into 3) in flour and set aside
3. Beat eggs with cheese and lemon juice
4. Heat oil over medium-heat. Cover chicken slices in flour, then egg batter. Place chicken in oil, cooking about 5 minutes on each side, until golden-brown
5. Add sliced lemon to pan, caramelizing one side and flipping on other side. Add garlic. Stir 1 minute
6. Add wine to pan. Pour in stock and bring to bubble
7. Slowly stir in seasoned butter, forming a sauce
8. Slide chicken back into pan to cook all the way through
9. Serve over linguine!

"In the center of the room, two of our tribespeople were dancing around the food that had been cooked for everyone. It was a custom that we did especially at large gatherings. Dancing around meant to celebrate life and each other; it was a way to show thanks to the world and nature around us."

-The Cursed Spirit 2

Margherita Pizza

Ingredients :

- 1 lb pizza dough
- 3-4 Roma tomatoes
- 2 garlic cloves
- 2 tsp oregano
- salt & pepper
- basil leaves
- mozzarella
- grated Romano cheese
- 1/4 cup corn meal
- Olive oil

Prep Time : 10 min

Cook Time : 15 min

Servings : 4-5

Procedure :

1. Preheat oven to 450F
2. Slice tomatoes and put in a bowl. Add crushed garlic, oregano, salt and pepper. Add olive oil and toss to marinate
3. While tomatoes sit to marinate, prepare pizza dough
4. Roll out pizza dough on floured surface into a round shape to fit your pizza pan
5. Place rolled out dough onto pizza pan that has been coated with corn meal
6. Brush olive oil on the dough. Layer shredded mozzarella cheese. Place tomato slices over mozzarella. Sprinkle grated cheese over tomatoes
7. Place in oven for 15 minutes. Put basil leaves over tomatoes while still hot
8. Enjoy!

Chicken & Shrimp Scampi

Prep Time : 10 min

Cook Time : 20 min

Servings : 4

Ingredients :

- 16 oz bag frozen shrimp (thawed)
- 2-3 chicken breasts (diced)
- 1 box angel hair pasta
- 14.5 oz Alfredo Sauce
- 1 tsp salt
- 2 tsp paprika
- 2 tsp italian seasoning
- 2 tbsp butter

Procedure :

1. In large pot, boil water on stove. Add angel hair pasta and allow to cook
2. In medium saucepan, melt 1 tbsp butter over medium heat. Add thawed shrimp (deshelled)
3. In another saucepan, melt 1 tbsp butter over medium heat. Add diced chicken breast
4. Cook both shrimp and chicken over medium heat. Add 1 tsp paprika and italian seasoning to both
5. Shrimp will be pink in color when cooked thoroughly. Take thickest piece of chicken out to cut and check that it is cooked and there is no pink left
6. Strain angel hair pasta and place back in pot. Add alfredo sauce to pasta, cooked chicken and shrimp
7. Stir Over low heat for about 5 minutes

*Note: Can sprinkle with romano or parmesan cheese to your heart's desire.

The Story of Gnocchi

The first time I ever tried gnocchi was actually when I went to study abroad in Italy. The pillowy potato pasta were such a comfort food that I knew I had to ask Nonni about as soon as I got home. You could have them with plain butter or tomato sauce. When Nonni and I went to visit Newburyport, MA, we walked into a cooking store. Within all of the store's items, I found a gnocchi roller.

"What are you going to end up getting?" Nonni asked me.

"This!" I showed her the gnocchi roller with pride.

"Oh, we always just used a fork. I've never seen that before!" Nonni said. "I can show you how to make it with a fork."

"I'm going to get this, Nonni. And then we can make it when we go back to Connecticut. And then years down the road I can teach my own children how to make gnocchi and tell them that I used this same tool with my Nonni," I said.

When we got back to Connecticut, I made mashed potatoes and we used the leftovers to make the gnocchi pasta. Nonni tried using the new tool that I got and ended up liking it so much that she used it on all the gnocchi she made.

Let's just say, we barely had any leftover it was so good.

Gnocchi

Ingredients :

- 2 large russet potatoes
- 2 large eggs
- 1- 1 1/2 cups flour
- 1/2 cup grated Parmesan or Romano cheese
- Salt & Pepper

Prep Time : 10 min

Cook Time : 5 min

Servings   : 4

Procedure :

1. Boil potatoes until tender. Make mashed potatoes according to your recipe (I like to use 1 tbsp butter and 1/4 cup milk depending on how many potatoes used)
2. Let mashed potatoes cook (This recipe can be done with leftover mashed potatoes)
3. Work eggs and cheese into mashed potatoes
4. Add flour a little at a time and work into the potatoes. If dough is sticky, add more flour to mixture.
5. Cut a small amount of dough and roll into ropes.
6. Cut into 1 inch pillows; using gnocchi tool or fork, press quickly angainst each "pillow" of gnocchi pasta and place on cookie sheet lined with parchment paper.
7. Boil gnocchi in salted water until they float to the top. Remove with strainer spoon to warm bowl.
8. Remove excess water from bowl and serve with your favorite sauce or buttered.

Turkey & Rice Meal Prep

Ingredients :

- 1 package ground turkey
- 1 cup jasmine rice
- 1 1/2 cups water
- 1 tbsp butter
- 3 tbsp taco seasoning
- 1 tbsp hot sauce
- 1 cup shredded cheddar cheese
- 2 roma tomatoes
- 1 avocado

Prep Time : 5 min
Cook Time : 15 min
Servings   : 4

Procedure :

1. In medium pot with lid, bring 1 cup jasmine rice, 1 tbsp butter and 1 1/2 cups water to a boil. Place lid on pot and turn heat down to low for 10 minutes
2. While rice is cooking, place ground turkey in medium saucepan and allow to cook on both sides, chopping with a wooden spoon as you turn over to cook all sides
3. Add taco seasoning and hot sauce when nearly cooked all the way through.
4. Add cooked rice to each meal prep container
5. Distribute cooked ground turkey throughout each
6. Add shredded cheddar cheese, diced roma tomatoes and sliced avocado. (May use lime or lemon juice over avocado to help preserve longer)

The smell of hot dogs and hamburgers filled the air in an aroma that reminded me of summertime get togethers way back when.

-The Cursed Monastery

Baked Ziti

Ingredients:

- 1 package ziti
- 2 cups mozzarella cheese
- 14 oz tomato sauce
- 2 tbsp italian seasoning

Prep Time : 15 min
Cook Time : 30 min
Servings : 5-6

Procedure:

1. Preheat oven to 350F
2. Boil ziti as directed on box
3. When cooked, strain ziti and pour half of the ziti in 13x9 cake pan
4. Pour half of the jar of tomato sauce over ziti
5. Using wooden spoon, carefully stir the sauce throughout
6. Sprinkle 1 cup of mozzarella over ziti in cake pan
7. Pour remaining ziti over and repeat steps 3-5 with remaining sauce and mozzarella
8. Top with italian seasoning
9. Bake for 30 minutes

Stuffed Peppers

Ingredients :

- 4-6 bell peppers (any color)
- ground turkey
- 1 cup jasmine rice
- 1 cup mozzarella cheese
- 1 can diced tomatoes
- 1/2 cup tomato sauce

Prep Time : 20 min

Cook Time : 30 min

Servings : 6

Procedure :

1. Set oven to 350F
2. Boil rice on stove
3. In medium saucepan, cook ground turkey, chopping into smaller pieces with wooden spoon
4. When cooked thoroughly, add can diced tomato. Stir and allow ground turkey to soak up the tomato juice
5. Pour cooked rice into ground turkey & tomato mixture. Stir thoroughly
6. Add 1/2 cup tomato sauce
7. Cut bell peppers in half, also cutting out the core and washing out the seeds
8. Place pepper halves in large pot of water on the stove to boil. Boil for about 5 minutes and strain. Place on cookie sheet
9. Fill each bell pepper half with ground turkey mixture and top with mozzarella cheese
10. Bake 30 minutes

Kielbasa & Potatoes

Ingredients :

- 14 oz polska kielbasa
- 3-4 potatoes (cooked)
- 1/2 onion
- 2 cloves minced garlic
- 1 tbsp butter
- 2 tbsp paprika
- 2 tsp salt
- 1 tsp pepper

Prep Time : 10 min

Cook Time : 20 min

Servings : 3-4

Procedure :

1. Cut kielbasa into slices
2. Melt butter in large saucepan, add kielbasa slices and cook on each side
3. Take kielbasa out and place in a bowl to add in later
4. Using the same saucepan, add in minced garlic and diced potatoes
5. Sprinkle paprika, salt, pepper and garlic
6. Cook until potatoes are a nice golden brown color
7. Add kielbasa back in and stir
8. Enjoy!

"Hey there, you may want to turn around and check the grill…" Sally came over and burst out laughing when he opened it up to let out a colossal poof of smoke in the air. He quickly turned the heat down a bit and flipped the burger patties and chicken wings onto the plate that Sally held next to him. She couldn't seem to stop laughing, but he felt so bad that he ruined the food.

-Presence

The Story of BBQ Chicken

Whenever my dad went out to cook on the grill and made chicken, it would always....always always have bbq sauce that it had been marinated in and mozzarella cheese melted perfectly over just at the last minute of cooking. For my entire life, this was just the "right way" to grill chicken. Without the mozzarella cheese or barbecue sauce, something always felt like it was missing entirely. Dad liked his chicken cooked almost to a crisp and I eventually ended up being the same exact way, but I'll always remember him walking out with the plate of raw chicken cutlets soaked in bbq sauce and bag of mozzarella cheese. His dog, Tinkerbelle, would follow him out back. Yes, he had a German Shephard named "Tinkerbelle." It doesn't get more vicious than that, if you ask me. But in all seriousness, he was a little bit mad at me for giving his dog a cartoon name. I'm not sure what else he expected though!!

"Slim, grab the spatula for me," he'd call in, knowing I was always eager to help in any way.

I got the spatula and another plate to put the chicken on when it was done. As soon as I got outside, he was giving a little piece to his dog and she gobbled it right up, forgetting she had even eaten anything, asking for more immediately.

"Me too, Tinkerbelle. Me, too," I had thought.

BBQ Chicken

Ingredients :

- 6-8 chicken cutlets, sliced thin
- 1/2 cup bbq sauce
- 1/2 cup mozzarella cheese
- salt & pepper to taste

Prep Time   : 5 min

Cook Time : 10 min

Servings   : 3-4

Procedure :

1. Place chicken cutlets in bowl with bbq sauce and salt & pepper. Allow to marinate for 2-4 hours
2. Place each cutlet onto the grill. Flip over and sprinkle with mozzarella cheese when nearly done
3. Take thickest cutlet out to cut and check if cooked thoroughly
4. Enjoy and dip in some bbq sauce!

Slow Cooked Chili

Ingredients :

- 1 package ground beef (2 lb)
- 2 cans red kidney bins
- 4-5 carrots
- 2 bell peppers
- 1/2 onion
- 2 cloves garlic, minced
- 2 tbsp tomato paste
- 1 tbsp cocoa powder
- 3 tsp cumin powder
- 3 tbsp chili powder
- 2 jalapenos (diced)
- 2 cans diced tomatoes
- 1 cup tomato sauce
- hot sauce
- sour cream
- shredded cheddar cheese

Prep Time : 15 min

Cook Time : 6-8 hours

Servings : 8-10

Procedure :

1. In medium saucepan, brown ground beef
2. When cooked thoroughly, strain beef and pour in slow cooker
3. Drain kidney bins and pour in slow cooker
4. Add sliced carrots, diced bell peppers, diced onion, garlic, tomato paste, cocoa powder, cumin powder, chili powder, jalapenos, cans of tomatoes, tomato sauce to slow cooker
5. Add hot sauce to your liking
6. Stir everything together in slow cooker
7. Cook on low for 6-8 hours
8. Serve with dollop of sour cream if you'd like and cheddar cheese sprinkled over

Chicken Parmigiana

Prep Time : 15 min

Cook Time : 20 min

Servings : 4

Ingredients :

- 1/2 lb raw chicken breasts, sliced thin
- Italian breadcrumbs
- 1 box angel hair pasta
- 1 jar tomato sauce
- 2 eggs
- 1 cup flour
- Shredded Mozzarella
- canola or vegetable oil
- Salt & pepper
- Paprika

Procedure :

1. Preheat oven 350F
2. Get large pot of water and boil angel hair pasta as directed on pasta box
3. Pour oil in medium size saucepan over medium heat
4. Prepare 3 medium sized bowls. Pour flour in one, whisk eggs in the second bowl and pour breadcrumbs in the third
5. Sprinkle salt, pepper & paprika over both sides of chicken
6. Using fork, place thinly sliced chicken breast in flour, covering both sides. Then, dip in egg mixture. Then, breadcrumbs
7. Place breaded chicken breasts in oil, flipping after 5 minutes or when side is a golden brown
8. When chicken is done, place on plate over a paper towel
9. In 13x9 pan, pour drained pasta in and lay cooked chicken cutlets over pasta. Pour tomato sauce over and sprinkle shredded mozzarella cheese to your liking. Bake for about 10 minutes

"Even though she was trained in gathering and cooking like the other women did, he would sneak late at night to teach her skills that would normally be taught to the boys of the tribe. One of the skills that she wanted to learn the most was hunting."

-The Cursed Spirit

The Story of Chicken Cutlet

Okay, if I died and went to heaven and could only eat one meal... it would be chicken cutlet and mashed potatoes. Don't get me wrong, it's delicious in every way and perfect. But what I think I like most about this dish is how traditional it is for me and my family. This was a "go to" dish my mom, dad and I had quite frequently. It was always so quick to make and you could do so much with it. If you made one meal of chicken cutlets, you could make chicken sandwiches with the leftovers or chicken parmigiana just by adding some sauce over it, slice it over some salad (for you salad eaters). There's just an unending list that you can do with it.

But what I love most about it was that it was a meal that I shared with my loved ones since I was little and it makes me feel comforted like I am still with them even when I am not. I'm sure we all have a meal like this in mind or something at the very least that makes us feel closer to home.

Chicken Cutlet

Ingredients :

- 1 package chicken breasts or tenders (sliced thin)
- 1 cup flour
- 2 eggs
- 1-2 cups breadcrumbs
- salt, pepper & paprika
- vegetable or canola oil

Prep Time : 10 min

Cook Time : 10 min

Servings : 4

Procedure :

1. Place medium sized saucepan on stove with 2 cups oil over medium heat
2. Sprinkle salt, pepper & paprika over both sides of chicken
3. Prepare 3 bowls. One with flour, second with whisked eggs and third with breadcrumbs
4. Using fork, coat both sides of each chicken with flour then dip in egg mixture then breadcrumbs, ensuring all sides are coated
5. Add 4-5 breaded chicken slices to saucepan at a time, flipping after about 5 minutes when side is golden brown
6. Take out and place on paper towel over plate
7. Enjoy next to some mashed potatoes!

The Story of Chicken Soup

"The Magical Chicken Soup," dad would joke with my mom.

My Great Grandpa Hiyi (he would always say aye-yi-yi so that's why his name is like that...story for another time) would always make chicken soup with fresh vegetables from his garden. The story of this chicken soup is mainly about him and his hard-working ways. Grandpa Hiyi was in Hungary when WW2 began. He hadn't even been able to finish elementary school. He fled to America where his sister lived and joined the military there, fighting against Nazis. He had met the woman who became his wife at church and she waited for him to come back from the war. He never did speak of the war much. It was too painful. And his wife, Martha, never pushed him to either. They eventually had three children and raised them with all the love in the world one could give. Martha unfortunately died before I was even alive and Grandpa continued doing what he knew best, making some of the best chicken soup one could ever make, taking care of his garden and his family.

Chicken Soup

Ingredients :

- 1 whole chicken
- 2 tbsp butter
- 4-6 cups water
- 32 oz chicken broth
- 2 tomatoes
- 2 stalks of celery
- 1 whole parsley root
- 5 carrots
- garlic powder
- 1 whole onion
- 1 1/2 tbsp salt
- 1/4 tbsp pepper
- 2 little pieces kolorabe
- 1/2 green pepper

Prep Time : 30 min

Cook Time : 3 hr

Servings : 6-8

Procedure :

1. Put butter in large pot on medium heat. When melted, place whole chicken carcass in pot to cook for about 5 minutes. (Make sure to take as much chicken meat off as you can to later add to the soup)
2. Pour in 4-6 cups water
3. Add whole diced onion, diced tomatoes, salt, pepper, parsley root and kolorabe to pot. Continue cooking at low heat for 1 1/2 hrs
4. Place large bowl in sink with strainer over it. Slowly pour out the soup and chicken carcass. Take chicken bones and discard. Add liquid back to the large pot and place back on stove
5. Add chicken broth and bring soup to a boil then reduce the heat
6. Add chopped celery, carrots and green pepper. Cook for an hour more. Serve with your choice of noodle

Pulled Chicken Tacos

Ingredients:

- 2-3 chicken breasts
- 2 tbsp butter
- 1 avocado
- 1 Roma tomato (diced)
- 1/2 cup shredded cheddar cheese
- 1/2 onion (diced)
- 2 cloves garlic (minced)
- Taco seasoning
- Hot sauce
- Sour cream

Prep Time : 10 min
Cook Time : 15 min
Servings : 4

Procedure:

1. Boil chicken breasts until cooked thoroughly. Drain and pour chicken in bowl. Using forks, pull chicken apart until it's in shreds
2. In medium saucepan, melt butter then add diced onion and minced garlic
3. Add pulled chicken
4. Put 3-4 tbsp taco seasoning over pulled chicken and hot sauce to your liking
5. Cook about 5-10 minutes, stirring throughout
6. Add spoonfuls of pulled chicken mixture to hard or soft shell tacos. Sprinkle cheese and diced tomato over
7. Top with diced avocado and a dollop of sourcream

Guacamole

Ingredients :

- 3-4 ripe avocados
- 2 Roma tomatoes
- 3 tbsp diced onion
- 2 garlic cloves (minced)
- 2 jalapenos
- 1 lime
- 1 tsp cumin
- salt & pepper

Prep Time : 10 min

Cook Time : 0 min

Servings : 3-4

Procedure :

1. Cut avocados in half and take pit out. Using spoon, remove avocado insides into bowl
2. Mash avocados with fork
3. Add diced tomatoes, onion, chopped jalaenos and cloves
4. Stir thoroughly
5. Add cumin, salt & pepper
6. Cut lime in half, squeeze each half into avocado mixture
7. Dip chips in and enjoy!

Pepperoni Bread

Ingredients :

- 1 lb pizza dough
- 1 egg
- sliced pepperoni
- shredded mozzarella

Procedure :

1. Preheat oven 375F
2. Roll out pizza dough on floured surface
3. Beat egg and brush over the dough (Save some egg to use as egg wash)
4. Start from the edge and place pepperoni slices over the dough then cover the pepperoni with a layer of shredded mozzarella
5. Roll from the longest side into a log shape. Brush egg on both ends before sealing. Brush the egg along the edge before sealing the dough
6. Place pepperoni log on a cookie sheet covered with parchment paper
7. Brush the remaining egg over the dough
8. Make small slits with a knife on top of the dough
9. Bake for 20 minutes or until golden brown in color

Prep Time : 10 min
Cook Time : 20 min
Servings : 6-8

Grilled Cheese

Ingredients :

- 2 slices of bread
- 2 bacon strips (cooked)
- 2 slices american cheese
- 2 tbsp butter
- 1 Roma tomato
- 2 spoonfuls bacon fat

Prep Time : 5 min

Cook Time : 5 min

Servings : 1

Procedure :

1. Over medium heat in small saucepan, put bacon fat in to heat up
2. Spread 1 tbsp of butter on each slice of bread
3. Place one slice of bread in pan, two pieces of cheese over and slices of bacon. Lastly, put 2 slices of tomato over that and other slice of bread
4. Flip with spatula and cook the other side until golden brown
5. Serve next to stop chips and enjoy!

Broccoli Casserole

Ingredients :

- 3 8 oz bags frozen broccoli
- 8 oz pack shredded sharp cheddar cheese
- 8 oz pack shredded mozzarella cheese
- 8 oz can cream of chicken
- 8 oz can cream of mushroom
- 2 boxes chicken stuffing (prepared)

Procedure :

1. Cook Broccoli. Drain. Place in 13x9 inch dish
2. Mix in cheese and cans of cream of chicken and mushroom
3. Put stuffing on top as top layer
4. Bake at 350 for 30 minutes

Prep Time : 10 min

Cook Time : 30 min

Servings : 6-8

Desserts

"We didn't do anything," I protested like a little boy that got his hands caught in a cookie jar."

-The Cursed Vessel

Wildberry Cobbler

Ingredients:

- 4 cups mixed berries (Blackberries, blueberries, strawberries)
- 2 cups sugar
- 1 tbsp lemon juice
- 2 tbsp cornstarch
- 1/4 tsp cinnamon
- 1 cup flour
- 1/2 cup brown sugar
- 1/2 tsp salt
- 1/2 tsp baking powder
- 1/2 tsp cinnamon
- 1 cup butter (chilled)

Prep Time : 10 min

Cook Time : 30 min

Servings : 8

Procedure:

1. Preheat oven 375 F
2. Combine berries, sugar, lemon juice and 1/4 tsp cinnamon in large bowl
3. Add cornstarch and cover berries. Pour into 9x9 in. baking dish
4. Combine flour, brown sugar, baking powder, salt and cinnamon in medium bowl
5. Cut in butter and use hands to make large crumbs form
6. Sprinkle evenly over berries in baking dish
7. Bake for about 30 minutes. (Golden brown crumbs and bubbling fruit)
8. Remove from oven. Let stand for at least 15 minutes
9. Serve with ice cream and enjoy!

Chocolate Chip Cookies

Prep Time : 1 hr 15 min

Cook Time : 8-10 min

Servings : 7-8

Ingredients :

- 1 cup butter
- 3/4 cup sugar
- 3/4 cup brown sugar
- 2 large eggs
- 1 tsp vanilla
- 1 tsp cinnamon
- 2 3/4 cups flour
- 3/4 tsp baking soda
- 3/4 tsp salt
- 2 cups chocolate chips

Procedure :

1. Preheat oven 350F
2. Mix butter, white sugar and brown sugar together until thoroughly mixed
3. Add eggs, one at a time and stir
4. Add vanilla, stirring throughout
5. In a separate bowl, stir all dry ingredients together
6. Slowly add dry ingredients to wet ingredients, stirring a little bit at a time
7. Fold in chocolate chips
8. Cover bowl and put in fridge for 1-2 hours
9. Drop by spoonful onto cookie sheet prepared with parchment paper
10. Bake 8-10 minutes, depending on size of cookies or until golden brown around edges

Peppermint Candy Cane Cake

Prep Time : 10 min

Cook Time : 45 min

Servings : 4-8

Ingredients :

- 1 box vanilla cake mix
- 1 tsp peppermint extract
- 6 candy canes
- egg
- oil
- red food dye
- 2 cups powdered sugar
- 3 tbsp whole milk
- 1 tsp vanilla extract

Procedure :

1. Prepare vanilla cake mix as directed on box
2. Pour about 1 cup of cake batter in separate bowl. Add peppermint extract and 2-4 drops of red food dye
3. Pour half of undyed cake batter in Bundt cake pan. Pour red dyed cake batter over that and then pour remaining undyed cake batter in Bundt pan
4. Bake as directed on cake box
5. Use knife to poke into cake and if comes out clean, the cake is cooked
6. Wait about 10 minutes to let cool and flip cake upside down on flat plate or serving plate
7. Whisk powdered sugar, milk and extract together in small bowl. Pour over cake
8. Crush two candy canes and place along outside of cake. Place remaining four candy canes in center of cake

Dog Treats

Ingredients :

- 2 1/2 cups Wheat flour
- 1 tsp baking powder
- 1/2 tsp cinnamon
- 1 cup peanut butter
- 1 cup water
- 2 tbsp honey
- 1 egg

Prep Time : 10 min

Cook Time : 15-20 min

Servings : 10

Procedure :

1. Preheat oven to 350F
2. Combine all dry ingredients in a bowl
3. Add egg, peanut butter, water and honey. Mix well
4. Roll out dough on floured surface to 1/2 inch thick
5. Use dog shaped cookie cutter to make shapes. Place biscuits on a cookie sheet lined with parchment paper
6. Bake for 15-20 minutes depending on size of the biscuit

Through the Generations

Nonni Rose & Nonni Maria

Nonni Rose taught me the power of patience and love for family. She would do anything for family no matter what. Some of my most fond memories are from sleepovers at her house even into adulthood and cozy nights in eating a festive popcorn creation she's cooked up with a movie. Our yearly trips each summer are something I always look forward to and I'm lucky I can call her my Nonni.

The fork and spoon from the opening page belonged to my Nonni Maria. She kept them on the wall in her kitchen as I do now. Certain smells such as oregano or even just homemade pasta sauce bring me back to Nonni Maria's kitchen no matter where I am. Despite the hardships she faced in her life, she always had a smile on her face and I aim to follow her example in life. She taught me that life is too short to get caught up on the little things.

Grandma NeeNee & Mom

Grandma NeeNee (because I couldn't say Jeanne) was the silliest person if you got to know her. She taught her grandchildren to throw spaghetti against the wall to see if it was cooked or not. She'd always play records or her radio while she cooked. I can still remember her humming along to the music. Grandma always dreamed of opening up a restaurant called "Papa Louis'" after her father and having recipes from around the world.

Mom, your broccoli casserole recipe finally got me to eat vegetables someway, somehow. Even if it meant eating most of the stuffing off the top and just a few pieces of broccoli. Thank you for letting me help around the kitchen growing up; I am fortunate to have learned from you and I hope to continue the tradition of Sunday chicken roasts in the oven.

In Loving Memory of...

Dad, I may have had to feed the scrambled eggs you made me to the dog (shhh, it's a secret), but there is one thing that you taught me and that was to keep trying no matter what and to never give up. On birthdays because you liked cake batter so much, I remember you'd tell me that you made me a cake only to open up the fridge and show me a bowl of the cake batter and hand me a spoon. When nonni made brownies, you'd sneak a spoonful of the batter and then run away as fast as you can and I've got to admit…I do the same and think you're probably laughing down from heaven. Dancing around the kitchen with you and playing pranks on mom never got boring. Life was a whole new adventure every day with you.

I love you 100,

Mitzes
(Because that's what I used to think my name was)

Milton Keynes UK
Ingram Content Group UK Ltd.
UKRC031512300924
449049UK00006B/33